Oceans

Yvonne Franklin

Oceans

Publishing Credits

Editorial Director
Dona Herweck Rice

Associate Editor
James Anderson

Editor-in-Chief
Sharon Coan, M.S.Ed.

Creative Director
Lee Aucoin

Illustration Manager
Timothy J. Bradley

Publisher
Rachelle Cracchiolo, M.S.Ed.

Science Consultants

Scot Oschman, Ph.D.
David W. Schroeder, M.S.

Teacher Created Materials

5301 Oceanus Drive
Huntington Beach, CA 92649-1030
http://www.tcmpub.com
ISBN 978-1-4333-0320-3
© 2010 Teacher Created Materials, Inc.
Made in China
Nordica.032015.CA21500127

Table of Contents

A World Beneath the Waves

There are worlds that very few people see. Some places have never been explored. Mysterious creatures roam there. Strange plants grow in tangles across the ground. Sometimes it is so dark that nothing can be seen.

What are these places? They are the oceans, of course. They are the world beneath the waves.

What Is It?

The ocean is the vast body of salt water that covers about 70 percent of Earth's surface.

Much of Earth's surface has been explored. But much of the land deep beneath the ocean's surface has not.

The Ocean Biome

Are oceans only large bodies of water? No, oceans are really much more than that. Oceans are **biomes** (BIE-ohmz). A biome is a large area of water or land. You can tell a biome by what you find there. Look at the land, plants, animals, and climate. These will show you what the biome is.

The main part of an ocean is the water. Oceans are made of salt water. That means there is a lot of salt in the water. You have probably tasted salt water if you have gone swimming at an ocean beach. Plants and animals that live in the ocean must be able to live in salt water.

So, is an ocean just a large body of water? No. It is everything that is below, on, and near its surface. All of this makes up the ocean biome.

Oceans are teeming with life.

Seas

Are seas the same as oceans? Yes and no. We often use the word *sea* when we mean ocean. But a sea is usually smaller than an ocean, and it is more surrounded by land.

Arctic Ocean

Atlantic Ocean

Pacific Ocean

Indian Ocean

Southern Ocean

Pacific Ocean

There are five oceans in the world. Some people say that they are really just one big ocean because they are all connected. Think of them like countries. Many countries are part of the same land. But we give them different names.

The largest ocean is the Pacific. It covers about one-third of the whole world! It makes up almost half of all the oceans. The smallest ocean is the Arctic. It is only about three percent of all the oceans. The other three oceans together are just a little bigger than the Pacific. They are the Atlantic Ocean, Indian Ocean, and Southern Ocean.

Southern Ocean

The Southern Ocean is also known as the Antarctic Ocean.

Antarctic ice caves along the Southern Ocean

Beaches

A beach is a place where the ocean meets the shore. It is often covered in sand. Sand is made of tiny bits of rock and shell. The sand of some beaches is so fine that it is soft underfoot. The sand from other beaches is larger. It can be rough under bare feet.

Beaches are part of ocean biomes. Many animals go back and forth from the water to the beach. Some animals lay their eggs on beaches. The hatched animals crawl to the water. Some birds get their food from both the water and the beach. They may rest on the sand. Some even rest on the water.

The water from the ocean washes back and forth on the beach. It pulls sand, animals, and even trash into the water. It washes things onto the shore as well. Be careful not to leave trash on a beach! It may wind up in the ocean. It will cause problems for living things there.

Tides

The level of water in an ocean goes up and down. That is because of **tides**. There is a high tide and a low tide every day. The tides are caused by gravity between Earth and the moon.

high tide

low tide

Tallest Cliffs

The tallest sea cliffs in the world are found in Kalaupapa, Hawaii. They are 1,010 meters (3,314 feet) tall.

Many animals make their homes on rocky ocean cliffs.

Cliffs

Cliffs are another place where the ocean and shore may meet. Cliffs are made where the ocean **erodes**, or wears away, the land. The rocky land is carved into a jagged wall. Cliffs can also be formed in the middle of oceans. Water erodes the land on all sides. Then the cliff towers up out of the waves.

Cliffs are a common part of an ocean biome. Many animals live on cliffs. Some birds keep nests there. Seals may lie on cliffs to rest in the sun.

Herons feed on the small fish they find in ocean bays.

Bays

The sun is always evaporating water from the ocean. That means the water is turning to vapor. Vapor rises into the air. Oceans would go dry if the water only turned to vapor. But new water flows into the oceans all the time. The water comes from rivers. It comes from rain and snow, too.

Rivers flow down to sea level. The mouth of the river widens near the ocean. This is called a **bay**. Dirt and sand from the river drop into the bay. That makes most bays shallow. Millions of small animals such as crab and shrimp live in this shallow water.

Amazon River

The Amazon River in South America is so large that it provides about 20 percent of all the river water that flows to the oceans.

Shallow Water

Ocean water near the coast is mainly shallow, or not deep. Most of the ocean's plants and animals live there. Sunlight can reach into the shallows to help living things grow. It is a good place for hunters to find **prey**. Animals that eat plants can find lots of food, too. The shallows are very busy!

Think of the shallows like this. If people lived in the shallows, the shallows would be cities. The open ocean would be the country.

starfish

Tide Pools

When the tide goes out, sometimes a pool of water stays behind. It is called a **tide pool**. Many small ocean animals, such as starfish, live in tide pools.

Reefs come in three main types: fringing, barrier, an
atoll. Fringing reefs form right around the shore.
Barrier reefs form around the shore but farther ou
Atolls are reefs that rise above the water while th
land sinks below it. It takes millions of years for a
fringing reef to become an atoll reef.

Coral Reefs

Coral reefs can be found in warm
waters near the coast. They are built
up across large rocks. Tiny coral
animals live there. They are called
polyps (POL-ips). Polyps have hard
skeletons and soft bodies. They
attach their skeletons to the rock and
to the skeletons of other polyps. The
skeletons are left behind when the
animals die.

Coral reefs are bright and colorful.
The **tentacles** (TEN-tuh-kuls) of the
polyps wave in the water. They look
like flowers. But they are not. Polyps
use their tentacles to catch food.

fringing

barrier

atoll

Jellyfish

Jellyfish float and swim without touching ground. Many can live deep down in an ocean. Some create their own light through a process called **bioluminescence** (bie-oh-loo-muh-NES-uhns).

Whales are among the largest creatures in the world. Some are the size of school buses!

Open Waters and Deep Below

Most of the ocean is wide-open water. Some of the biggest and smallest living things are found there. **Plankton** (PLANGK-ton) is made up of such small living things that they cannot be seen. But giant whales eat that food.

Deep below the surface is the ocean floor. Mountains, valleys, and plains are there. Most of the floor is cold and dark. Light cannot reach past 500 meters (1,640 feet). Strange creatures live there. Some glow in the dark for light. Others have super eyesight or move by touch or sound.

Most of the ocean floor has not been explored. It is too big and hard to reach. Scientists always look for new ways to see what is happening there.

plankton

Ocean Life

The ocean is a biome. So, it is filled with plants and animals. There are many **species** (SPEE-seez) there. They are big, small, and every color. They swim, float, walk, and fly.

Many species live together. They live in an **ecosystem** (EK-oh-sis-tuhm). An ecosystem is made of plants, animals, water, land, and air. The living things in an ecosystem help each other to survive. They use the water, land, and air.

All animals need to breathe. Some ocean animals breathe air. But some breathe under the water. They use **gills** to do it.

sea otters

Take a Breath

How long can you hold your breath? Some whales can hold theirs for more than an hour!

22

polar bear

dolphin

The oceans are home to more than 170,000 species of animals.

Barreleye Fish

The barreleye fish looks ahead when it is grabbing a bite of food. But most of the time it looks straight up. How does it look up? Its head is **transparent**, and it can turn its eyes 90 degrees!

The photo shown here was taken by the Monterey Bay Aquarium Research Institute (MBARI). Scientists at the MBARI study sea life and work hard to protect it.

Uses for Algae

People use algae in many things. It is a common ingredient in paint, ice cream, toothpaste, and more!

One of the most common living things in the ocean is **algae** (AL-jee). People used to think algae is a plant. But it is not. Scientists now know that most algae are small life forms that are similar to plants but are not plants.

Kelp is a kind of algae. It grows in shallow water. It can grow tall across large areas. Little bubbles in the kelp help to keep it upright.

The most important plants in the ocean are tiny. They are called **phytoplankton** (fayh-tuh-PLANGK-tuhn). *Phyto* means plant. *Plankton* means drifter. Phytoplankton just drifts along. It is like the grass of the ocean. Many ocean animals eat it.

The plants of the ocean are important to all animals. They give the world more than half of its oxygen.

kelp forest

Move It!

Ocean animals move in many ways. The nautilus swims backwards. Crabs walk sideways. Whales flap their tails. Squid squirt water to push themselves along.

nautilus

whale

Protect the Oceans

Oceans are important. We count on them for many things. We eat the fish that live there. We breathe the oxygen that ocean plants make. We move people and cargo in boats across the ocean. We take energy from ocean water and wind. People play in the ocean, too.

Pollution is a big threat to oceans. It kills animals and plants. It makes the water harmful for people. Too much fishing harms the ecosystem.

People must protect the oceans. They must think about how their actions affect the oceans. Healthy oceans help to keep the whole planet healthy.

A work crew cleans a harmful oil spill.

Lab: Climate Adaptati

Biomes are areas of land with similar climates, landscapes, animals, and plants. The living things in a biome depend on climate for their survival. When climates change, plants and animals must adapt, or change, to survive.

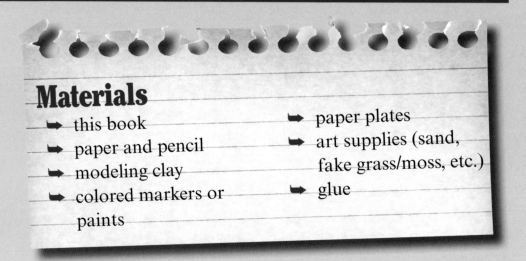

Materials
➡ this book
➡ paper and pencil
➡ modeling clay
➡ colored markers or paints
➡ paper plates
➡ art supplies (sand, fake grass/moss, etc.)
➡ glue

Procedure:

1. Select one plant and one animal from this reader's biome. Think about their physical features. What adaptations do they have that help them survive?

2. Record this plant and animal and their adaptations in the first two columns of the table shown on the next page.

3. Imagine this plant and animal were taken to a new biome with a different climate. How might they adapt to survive?

4. Write your ideas in the third column of the table.

5. Use clay and paint to create a model of the adapted plant and animal.

6. Use a paper plate to create your new biome. Color the plate and glue other art supplies to it to make it look like the new biome.

7. Place the clay models you created in their new biome.

8. Write a paragraph describing the plant and animal you chose. Explain how the adaptations you added will help them survive in their new biome.

Plant/Animal Name	Biome: _____ Adaptations	New Biome: _____ Adaptations
Animal Name		
Plant Name		

Glossary

algae—water-living organisms

bay—the large mouth of a river, also called an estuary

bioluminescence—the production of light by living organisms

biome—a complex community that is characterized by its common plants, animals, and climate

coral reefs—ridges of rock and hardened animal skeletons at or near the surface of the water

ecosystem— a geographical area where plants, animals, land, and weather all interact

erodes—wears away through the activity of water or wind

gills—the organs used by some marine animals to breathe

phytoplankton—tiny plants in the ocean that just drift in the water

plankton—microscopic organisms that drift in fresh or salt water and are eaten by fish and other ocean life

polyps—a type of animal with a mainly fixed base, a column body, a mouth, and tentacles

prey—something that is hunted for food

species—a group of living things with common characteristics or of the same type

tentacles—flexible limbs used for feeling, grasping, and movement

tide—the rise and fall of ocean waters twice each day

tide pools—pools of water left on the shore when the tide goes out

transparent—able to be seen through

Index

Scientists Then and Now

Dorothy Hill
(1907–1997)

Francisco Dallmeier
(1953–)

As a child in Australia, Dorothy Hill did very well in school. She impressed her family and teachers and received many special awards. In college, she chose to study geology because she could study it while out in nature. She became an expert on corals. Later, Hill became the first female college professor in Australia. She was also the first female president of the Australia Academy of Science.

Francisco Dallmeier has always been curious about birds. He studied all about them in school. He learned so much that he became the head of a museum. That was when he was just 20 years old! He is now one of the people in charge at the Smithsonian Institute. It is one of the biggest museums in the world. He runs the museum's research on plants and animals.